THIS BOOK

Belongs to

....

COLOR TEST

HARVESTER

DIGGER

DUMP TRUCK

TRACTOR

TRUCK

TRACTOR WITH PLOW

BULLDOZER

EXCAVATOR TRUCK

TRACTOR MOVER

FORKLIFT

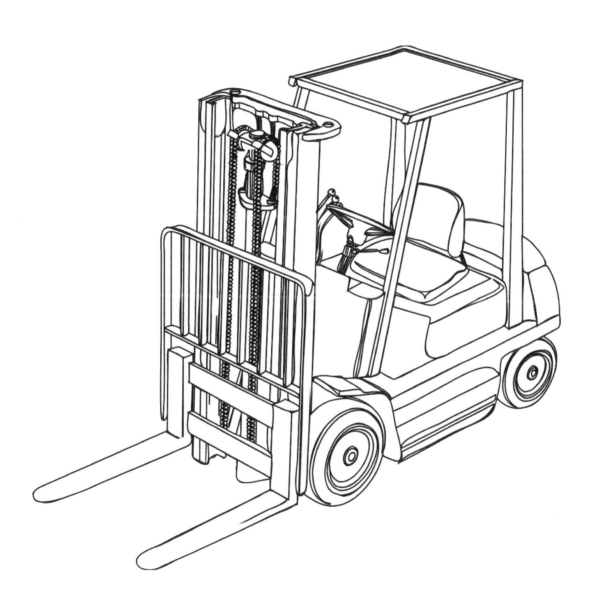

CEMENT TRUCK

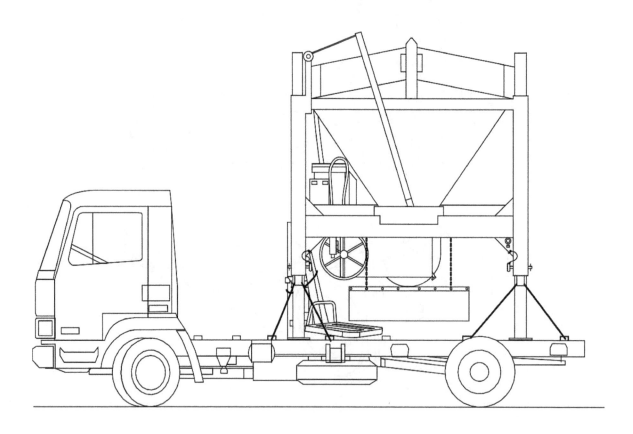

TRACKED EXCAVATOR

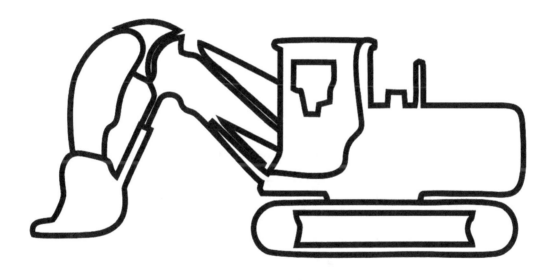

BULLDOZER ON WHEELS

ROAD ROLLER

DUMP TRUCK

EXCAVATOR

BACKHOE LOADER

CRANE

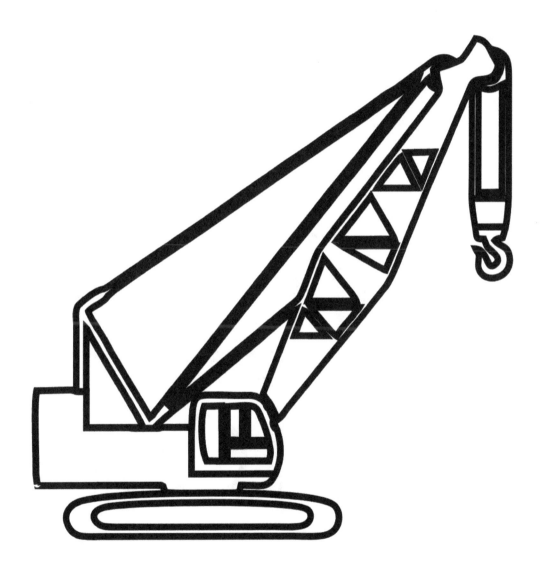

BULLDOZER ON WHEELS

ROAD ROLLER

CRANE ON WHEELS

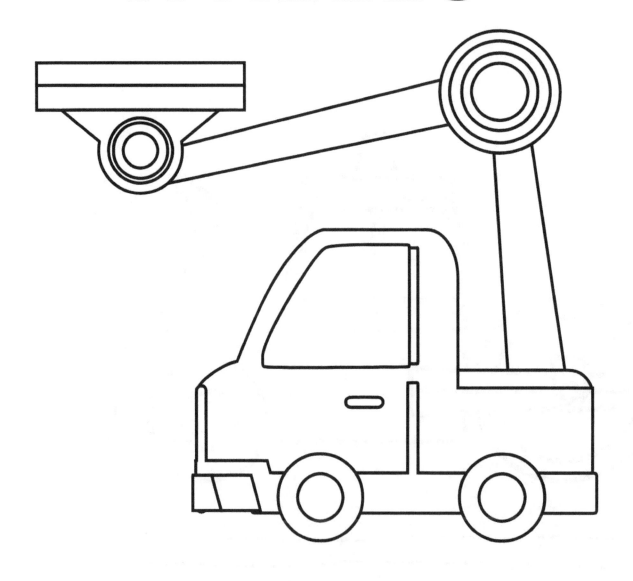

www.ingramcontent.com/pod-product-compliance
Lightning Source LLC
LaVergne TN
LVHW070831281224
800066LV00014B/1253